The Re

(The guide to the path of Self-Realization)

By Roshan Sharma

ISBN-978-93-5267-410-7.

Dedication

Before I initiate with the dedication part, let me share this truth of life. No matter what you achieve or attain with life, your life is incomplete without the people around you.

With life, you need people. Whether, its family, friends, colleagues, neighbours, or relatives but life is just not possible, without the love of the people around you.

The people are the real life force behind your success. If you think, you don't have the real people around you, then you have to look for them and create a circle of right people around you. In my case, I was fortunate enough to have people around me that helped me to achieve, whatever little or more I have attained in my life.

First and foremost, I would like to acknowledge and give my respect to my masters, Brahmakumaris (Organization), Osho, Shri. S.N. Tavariaji and every person who served me on my path called life.

God would have remained a far-fetched thing for me, if I have not encountered my masters in one or the other form, on my journey called life.

I am deeply indebted to all my masters, and share my heart-felt gratitude, with all the gestures possible.

Moving forward, I just cannot miss to acknowledge my family, friends, and all those people knowingly or unknowingly supported me on my path, to help me reach, where I am today.

From the bottom of my heart and with all the honesty, I can say that I have experienced god, and for the rest of my life, I will be fully devoted to him.

On the path of self-realization, you always walk with added responsibility. It's not that your life belongs to others, but it's also true that everyone who exists on earth belongs to you.

You just cannot differentiate yourself from any person who exists on earth.

You become part of everyone and everyone becomes part of you.

With the realization of the self, the primary instinct that you receive from within is to share. Whatever you receive from life, you have to share with others.

You just cannot keep it with yourself. You have to give as much as possible and serve others to bring them closer to their real self.

There are always people waiting for your guidance. Every person who walks down this earth holds the craving inside to experience god.

After the realization of the self, your responsibility remains, is to serve those who are ready to encounter god and needs a little guidance, so that they too can experience the absolute truth within.

Love & Respect,

Roshan Sharma.

Table of Contents

Preface

Sometimes the reflection is enough to guide you towards the truth. If there is a dust on your face, all you need is a mirror that can reflect the dust. Once the dust is reflected, you don't need somebody to tell you to wash your face, but you know what to do with your face.

The same applies with the ultimate truth of life. Once you know the truth, then you don't need anybody to tell you what to do with it. You live it and make it a part of your life. You see the difference between your present life and the truth, and you do everything to cover the difference.

Life is all about living the truth, but unless we realize it for ourselves, we simply remain engaged with the illusory part of life. The illusion is not the external reality, but the illusion is our own perception towards life. It's

11

our perception that creates our life. If our perception is far away from the truth, then we build our life on illusory perceptions.

Truth liberates. With the realization of truth, the false drop from life. With the truth, you just cannot associate with the things that lead to illusion. Your path and destination change with the truth.

The mind thinks that life starts and ends with the identity of the mind. For the mind, no truth exists beyond itself. However, when the mind itself experiences the truth beyond its limited perception, and figure out its own source of life, then all the preconceived notion of the mind sheds away.

Every mind has his individual perception to view the world. No other truth exists for the mind than the perception it carries for life. When the mind experiences life beyond itself, all the

12

thinking, and imagination of the mind gets drop, and the mind becomes the observer of life.

The mind can disturb you to the point where the ego or personal identity of the mind exists. Once the source of the mind itself is realized inside, than the mind stops to interfere with its unusual nature and co-operate to understand the true nature of the life.

The effort through this book is to give you the reflection of the truth. Once your mind can understand what truth is, it will be easier for your mind to move towards the truth.

Before you experience something in your life, your mind needs to know, that such kind of experience exists in you. Once the mind understands the reality behind the truth, it holds the power to bring you closer to the realization of truth.

All the effort with the book is to give your mind the direct experience of truth, so that whenever the quest for the truth arise in you, your mind already knows, on which path it has to lead you, so that you too can experience the truth.

1. **Eternal circle of Life**

The eternal circle of life is the cycle of birth and death. Do we repeat the cycle of birth and death and if we do, what happens after death, or how we choose our birth?

These few puzzles of life haunt the mind all the time. The mind can no way figure out the truth behind it.

When it comes to the eternal circle of life, the mind cannot understand the daily life to be the eternal circle of life, but for the mind, the eternal means some ever-lasting magic of out of the world has to happen to experience the eternal moment of life.

The eternal truth is certainly hidden from the mind, but this doesn't mean the mind doesn't have an access to it. On top of that, the eternal circle of life is no different from your day-to-day life. The time you realize the ultimate truth in you, the day-to-day process of life will become the eternal circle of life.

You will realize that your everyday life itself is the process of life, but you are nowhere connected with it. Your mind is not connected with your day-to-day life. Your mind is always somewhere in the past or working for the future.

The eternal circle of life is happening in this moment. The whole process of life is to connect with this very moment of life, so that, you experience the eternal circle, not somewhere in the heaven, but here and now, in this moment.

As to dreams and desires are the nature of the mind, in a similar way, to know the eternal truth, is also the nature of the mind. The beginning and end of life happen within the mind.

After the self-realization, the external reality remains the same, but you realize the truth behind the eternal life.

You realize how you come to this body and how life exists in the existence. This truth of life liberates you from all the bondage of life and makes you one with the eternal circle of life.

Life repeats itself every day. Day follows the night and night follows the day. This is an eternal circle of life. To connect with the eternal circle of life, you have to connect with life on a daily basis.

Just by understanding the repetitive process of day and night will give you the glimpse of the eternal circle of life. Either you move back before 5000 years ago, or you think for the future after 100, 200 or 500 years, one circle that is constant is the circle of day and night.

If your mind can understand this eternal circle of life, it becomes easier for your mind to move towards the deeper truth of life.

It's impossible for the mind to hold itself with the circle of day and night. The mind is so engrossed with its own past and future, that it doesn't have time to know the truth behind itself.

You put your mind to anything, and it will reveal the secrets of life to you. You have to look within and ask yourself what you are looking with life.

The life is ever-present in this moment, but it's the mind that runs in the past and the future always running away from the natural process of life. If you can simply observe your life for twenty-four hours of the day, you will notice the shift inside.

The physical reality that you perceive with the mind is just fine for the external use. The physical reality is good for utility purpose, but you cannot create your life around it. The life of the human can take place with much bigger dimensions. When you perceive the external world through the senses, you perceive the external world in your mind. Your mind creates a perception of the external reality, either out of your experiences and impressions of life or out of your understanding towards life.

The external reality comes out of the natural process but when you see the external reality, you cannot see the natural process behind it, but your perception remains limited to the limitations of your mind.

Let say you live in a 100 years old house, build by your grandfather. Now, when the third person sees the house, it sees the house as an old constructed property. However, when you see the same house, you have all your feelings and emotions attached to it.

The same applies to life as a whole. Any part of your life, you only see with your limited perception but not keeping whole view in mind. This restricts your perception to your individual mind and you separate yourself from the whole. Life works as a whole, but with the individual mind, you separate yourself from the whole.

The individual mind only sees the external reality with the attachment and thus, it cannot see the actual truth behind it. When you see the house, out of your attachment, you cannot see the actual reality of the house. The house stands because of its build up before 100 years ago, and with the time, it will fall. Your perception only allows you to see the house with your memories with the house.

Your memory in your mind is separate from the house. Your memory is the memory of your

20

mind. To experience life as a whole, you need to understand the perception of your mind. Your perception is nothing but the past memories. The memory of the mind is you accumulate out of experience. When you take your attention inward, you can look into your own memories that you have accumulated over the time, and rise above it.

If you can understand that, anything that exists in the external reality, not only the house, but anything that is physical is just another build up, and will fall with the time, or will be replaced by another build up, then you can separate yourself from anything that exists as physical in the physical reality.

You don't have to separate yourself from the physical things that belong to you, but at-least you can understand the actual truth behind it.

The next thing that needs to be understood is the memories of the mind. Now, the memories that you hold for the external reality, either it's the house, or the person, or the situation or any events of your life is just the memory of your individual mind, and it has nothing to do with the whole truth.

The whole truth is separate from the memory of the mind. The memory of the mind only belongs to the individual mind, and the memory along with the time will be replaced by fresh memories. If this little truth is understood by the mind, then slowly you can separate yourself from the memories, and see your thoughts and images of the mind as detached observer.

The physical reality is temporary and even the memories of the mind are temporary and is replaced with time. Thus, we have to look for something in us that is beyond the temporary physical reality and the subtle memories. Unless we figure out that truth in us, at least we can try to understand the physical and subtle world.

22

This will help us to move into the deeper reality of life and brings us closer to our real authentic self.

To connect with the eternal circle of life, that is ever-present in the moment, you don't have to die, but you have to realize the self, that exists beyond the physical and subtle world. The self is the source of life. The self exists in you, beyond the memories of the mind. The self is nothing but the mind without memories. The pure state of mind is the self.

The experience of a pure state of mind is liberation. The truth liberates. The truth allows you to directly look into life, either of the physical or subtle world.

You only experience yourself separate from the eternal process of life, because of your understanding. You never use your understanding to search for the truth, but accept whatever you see in the physical world. Your present life is far away from the truth. You only live the external reality, but never try to look for the internal truth.

Life is happening all the time. It doesn't matter either you exist or not, but life still happens. When you allow this thought to sink deep inside, you try to see life, beyond your personal identification. Try to understand life, dropping your personal identification with it.

How do you see your personal life, if you don't exist?

Life will still happen. If life can still hold itself, without you then what is the reason of your existence? Why do you exist?

Understanding with life can only happen if you learn to drop yourself. Don't try to see and understand life from your perspective, but drop all the perspective and see the natural flow of life. By observing, the natural flow of life you realize the truth.

With the cosmic universe, your intention is enough to connect with the eternal circle of life. Even if you don't understand anything about life, but if you hold the intention to know life, life will reveal itself to you.

With life all you need is patience in the moment. It's the present moment that reveals everything about life. You wish to know something of the outside world or you wish to know the deeper secrets of the inner world, it's always the present moment, where you realize the truth.

The circle of life works with the cause and effect. The cause and effect moves in a circle. With life, if the cause comes out of you, you experience the effect of it. Both cause and effect are part of you.

Let see in detail how cause and effect actually works with life.

2. Cause and Effect with Life

You are the cause and everything is an effect. This truth needs to be understood. Nothing can exist in your life, if at any point of time; you have not created the cause for it. Your life is just an effect. Cause has already been created in the past and you go on creating the cause of which you experience the effect.

Anything that you experience in the external world in the form of situation, people, or events in your life comes out of the definite cause you create inside of you. You never see yourself as the cause, or you never try to look for the cause inside of you, and thus you miss to understand even the effect.

If you try to understand life only out of the effect, then you only try to understand whole life from the half-truth. The cause of the physical world exists in the subtle world, and the cause of the subtle world exists in the source of the subtle world, i.e. life energy. The life happens deep in you and you only experience the effect of it, and define your conclusions out of it. Your conclusions can never be closer to the truth, unless you experience the whole truth in you.

With life, one thing that works perfectly in synchronization is cause and effect. For every cause, there is an effect. The cause and effect follows the circle of life. The life doesn't follow the rule of karma, but the life follows the rule of cause and effect. Life is science, whereby nothing in the universe happens by luck, chance, or fate. For your every experience of life, you hold the cause in you.

If you are the cause of life, then only you hold the power to change your life. If the cause is not in your hands, then you don't hold any control over your life. The change in life comes by working on your cause. Your daily living is the

28

cause of your life. The effect you see in the form of experience. Your daily habits are the cause of your life. You cannot receive anything other than what you have offered to life.

The external reality is a mere reflection of what you carry inside of you. The external world simply reflects what you hold in your subtle world. Remember the external reality only reflects your perception towards life. The external reality simply reflects your mind in different situations, moments, and experiences of your life. If you go on making the choice, without understanding its consequences, you are bound to create a mess with your life. Unless you see the cause and effect of the action, you cannot have clarity with life.

To see the cause and effect means to have clarity with life. You don't jump to life, but you see the process of life in advance. You just don't form the desire, but you see the consequence of

29

it. You know where you are heading with life. The cause and effect allow you to remain alert every moment.

The life follows a clear process of cause and effect. A certain process will derive a certain result. Before you create a cause, the effect has to be clear in your mind. Once the effect is clear, you can adjust your cause. Remember the cause needs to be adjusted according to the effect. The cause exists because of the effect. The effect is the result.

The cause is your energy, thoughts, feelings, and actions. For a certain effect, you need to adjust the cause. The right cause results into right effect. You cannot be rigid with the cause. Once the effect is clear, the cause can be adjusted as many times, as possible.

Say for e.g., you wish to reach the destination on the north side. Then your journey has to be on the north side. You cannot move on the south,

30

and expect yourself to reach to the north side destination.

This happens with many. You can only fail with life if your cause is not alignment with the effect. Life is all about experiment. You have to have an open mind. You have to open for an experiment as many times as possible. Your actions are the experiment and your expected result, allows you to adjust your action plans.

Say, if you are looking for a child. To have the child, we all know the process. The child is an effect of the process. You get into the cause to create an effect. To have a definite effect, you need to have a definite cause.

The cause is an entire process. The cause is not a single choice or decision, but the cause is the whole process that reaps the result. Understand the whole process that will result into an effect. The cause is not merely a choice or decision, but the whole process. You don't

31

manifest your desire, out of single choice, but you have to understand the process and stay with the process.

The full-fledged tree is an effect, but the cause lies in not only sowing the seeds but also going through the entire process of nourishing and taking care of the seed until it reflects as a tree.

When you imagine things in your mind, you see the effect. When you form dreams and desires in your mind, then dreams and desires are the effects. However, the effect only becomes your reality, if your mind can also imagine the whole process to produce the effect. The cause is the entire process that produces the effect.

Now onwards when you dream or create desires, just see do you only create desire, or along with it, you also create the path that takes you towards your desires.

If your mind creates both the path and the desires, then your thinking process is right, but if you only dream things, but don't know how to get to the dreams, then your dream will never turn into a reality. All the dreams and desires need a definite path for its manifestation in the physical reality.

You may not see the whole path, but at least one-step is required to move towards your dreams. If you know how to take that one-step, then the further step will be created on the path. Many people don't hold the courage to walk till the end. They give up in the middle of the path. They look for the shortcut. The failures are hard to digest for many. Not everyone can digest the failures with life.

What you experience today is the effect of living from the past. You cannot change what exists, other than to accept. Your today is the result from yesterday. You cannot change yesterday but you can accept it whole-heartedly. If you don't like what you experience it today, work on today, to experience the different reality in the future.

The mind has been trained to think only in the context of effect. People think in the form of result, but they don't even consider the action plan, or the path that will derive the result. Your path takes you to the destination, and your present destination, gives you the detail about the path that you have travelled.

Say, the person got the disease. Now, he will do everything to cure the disease. To work on the disease is to work on the effect. You take medicines to cure the disease, but you never get into the cause of it. If the disease is minor, it ultimately goes away by itself, but if the disease is major, you spend your whole life taking medicines for the disease, but never try to get into the cause of it.

34

Working on the cause of the disease is not curing the disease, but eliminating the disease forever from your life.

To work on the disease is to work on the effect. The disease is the effect of your particular way of life. The way of living is the cause of your disease. Your daily living is not limited to your daily actions, but it also includes, what you think and feel whole day. The cure is important to stabilize the disease so that the disease doesn't grow, but the real work is needed on the cause. The cause is the way of living. It's the way of living that keeps you healthy.

The mind can hold only one desire. Either you can live with the desire for the worldly life or you hold the desire for the truth. With the worldly desires, you drop the truth, but when you strive for the truth, even the external reality, is included on the journey towards the truth.

The process of cause and effect doesn't follow the mind, but it follows the inner movement of life energy. Unless you realize the life energy inside and get used to its movement, it's not possible to become one with the natural process of cause and effect. Cause and effect is not separate, but it's only one. One follows another. The cause follows the effect and the effect again turns itself into a cause, unless you bring your awareness to it, and begin to make necessary changes with it.

The life towards the self is to move towards the cause of life. The external reality is all about experiencing the effect while the journey towards the self, is to move towards the cause of life and rise above it.

Let see what you can expect on the spiritual path, as the mind already holds lots of illusion, about the spiritual path.

3. Life on the Spiritual Path

Does the life on the spiritual path is different, from your daily life?

The answer is both yes and no. In a way life is life, and it doesn't differ either you are living the worldly life or you walk on the spiritual path. On the other hand, there is something in you begins to unfold. You come closer to the existential truth of life. If your inner world opens up, you begin to perceive life in a different way.

In a way, nothing changes, but on the other hand, everything changes for you. You just cannot perceive life the way others see, but you receive altogether a different eye to perceive the world.

Both the inside and outside life becomes clear to you. The spiritual path is where your life unfolds. You come closer to the truth. Life happens as usual in the outside world, but inside you develop the art to observe. You don't interfere but you allow the life to unfold. You understand the natural unfoldment of life. The life unfolds in you. This is what Buddha has described as reversing the wheel of karma.

All that you have lived begins to unwind on the spiritual path. There are two ways to go about life. One way is to actively participate in life. You create dreams and desires, and you go on chasing them, and once one desire is fulfilled, you create bigger and better desire that keeps you engaged with life. You spent your whole life chasing different desires.

The other way to go about life is to live life out of understanding.

You follow the way of chasing the desire, but then in the middle of the path, you realize that this way will not take you to the ultimate

38

fulfilment, and thus you look for the different path.

Then you opt for the way of understanding. You don't simply run but you understand. You understand yourself. You understand the ways of life. You understand the actual need of life. You figure out, the actual purpose of life, and direct your energy in that direction. The personal and professional life remains as it is, but your perception begins to shift inward.

The spiritual path is all about the inner shift. On the spiritual path, you see what serves the purpose of life and the things that are not useful on your path. All your dreams, and desires and experiences of life are borrowed stuff from outside.

The imagination is not the reality of life, but the reality is that, which you are experiencing in this moment. This very moment of life is eternal. This moment is reality, and not what goes in your mind. Can you hold yourself to this moment?

Only on the spiritual path, your life appears to be more authentic. The spiritual path is where you come closer to the truth. Where you don't accept your reality that your mind shows you, but you look directly into the present life. You negate your thinking and imaginative part of the mind and directly experience life in the moment.

You don't have to be somewhere else to know the truth, but wherever you are, just with the intention to know the truth, you can direct your energy towards the truth.

When you create an intention to know the truth, the situation, people, or events will arrange itself, to give you a glimpse of the truth. Slowly your mind and energy will begin to move inward. It will be hard for the mind to understand, but everything will happen on its own.

40

You will observe life more rather to actively participate in life. Slowly you will realize the ways of life. The spiritual path reflects your life. More and more you reflect back, more and more you lose meaning out of it, and you begin to find the way in the natural unfoldment of life.

You notice the unnecessary struggle with life and realize that the simple understanding is enough to allow the life to happen. No force or effort is required with life, but your presence in the moment is enough for the natural unfoldment of life.

The spiritual path is the path towards the source. The source in you is the ultimate intelligence. When you move towards the source, your understanding grows about life. You understand how life unfolds in you and in the outside existence.

The spiritual path connects you with the self.

Every moment of life is interconnected. One thing leads to another. Life is not divided outside, but it's divided in the mind. The mind divides life as personal, professional, or spiritual life. For the first time, when you will realize life beyond mind, you notice that there is only life. No personal, professional, or even spiritual life exists but all the bifurcations exist only in the mind. On the spiritual path, you don't look for the mundane or repetitive process, but life moves to the unknown.

The spiritual path is an unknown path. The mind can never hold its past or future on the spiritual path. For the mind, every experience is experienced for the first time on the spiritual path. On the spiritual path, you grow each day from within. You want to understand everything that happens in your life.

All the scarcity and fear lies in the mind. The more you understand life, the more you get in tune with the abundant flow of life.

Life on the spiritual path is a conscious life. You become more conscious of everything that you do and everything that happens in the moment.

The mind not knowing the truth remain engaged in the mind-made reality, simply rotating in a circle of subtle and physical world. However, when the attention of the mind comes to the moment, it breaks the repetitive patterns of life and you slowly begin to rise above it. The karmic cycle of life gets break with the awareness in the moment.

Your mind is pure awareness field. When you fill your mind with all the unnecessary stuff, your awareness in the moment gets dim. When you go on dropping all the unnecessary stuff from the mind, your awareness expands in the moment.

We all are filled with lots of garbage from inside. The process of life is simple but the garbage within us doesn't allow us to experience life in its true color.

Remember you are the one, who gives color to life with your perception, and your perception depends on what you carry inside. When you are over-filled with unnecessary things, your perception with life also reflects the same.

The whole process on the spiritual path is to empty yourself from inside, so that natural life can flow from within.

There are certain tools that can be useful to empty yourself from inside. Meditation is one of the tools that can serve you for the inner cleansing process.

Life has a certain process, and it follows its process. When your mind is engaged in the external reality, you do nothing but fill yourself up with different experiences and impressions of the external life.

With the outward attention you learn to fill yourself up, but you never figure out the method to empty yourself from inside.

Your whole life is spent in filling the void of your inner world, but you never give a thought to look into your inner world.

The inner world seems absolutely empty, but that's not the reality. It's only the inner world that allows you to experience life outside.

The time you make conscious effort to move inward, even the truth of the inner world begins to reveal to you.

The practice of meditation is one such tool that can give you a direct access of your inner world.

What Meditation does?

In the process of meditation, you learn to observe life. You spare few hours each day, to consciously observe your life. You develop your presence in the moment. You not only see the circle of the past, but you also figure out the way to break the circle, and realize the ultimate truth of life.

Let see what meditation is, and how it can bring you closer to the self.

4. What is Dhyana or Meditation?

Before you understand what meditation is, be clear with where you are heading towards with meditation. Meditation leads to the purest state of mind.

What is the purest state of mind?

The purest state of mind is the state, where your mind is free from the past and future. The state of mind that can directly look into the process of life.

When the ignorant looks at the world, he only perceives life out of the perception of his mind. Not only that but for him, that's the only truth exist in life. For him, no other truth exists other than the perception of his mind.

The process of meditation connects you with your truth. In the first place, you realize your own perception of the mind. Only when you realize, how you perceive life, space is created inside, to perceive life beyond the individual perception.

Meditation is a mystery to many. It seems like everyone knows meditation, but when they sit with themselves, they don't know what to do with the word call meditation.

What to do in meditation or how to meditate is the biggest query of all.

Before you get into meditation, at least basics need to be clear about the meditation. The meditation is a tool or technique to realize the source of life. This is the purpose of meditation. The practice of meditation can reveal all the mysteries of life to you.

Meditation is not just another technique, but meditation holds the power to make you one with life.

How to practice meditation?

48

The practice of meditation begins with the observance. With the daily course, when you perceive life, you cannot see the truth of the moment, but you only perceive out of the perception of the mind.

When you observe the external reality, you get familiar with the external surroundings. You bring your mind to the external environment. You allow your mind to get familiar with the external environment.

It takes some time for the mind to settle with the external environment. When your mind gets settle with the external environment, naturally you can observe the movement of the inflow and outflow of breath.

Your mind can observe the external environment along with the inflow and outflow of breath.

You bring all your attention from outside to the inflow and outflow of breath. If your mind gets in tune with the inflow and outflow of breath, slowly you can close your eyes, and observe the movement of your breath.

The breath moves deep inside the body and flows out. You observe the depth of the breath. You allow your mind to follow the breath and make sure the attention of the mind doesn't deviate from the breath.

Slowly as your mind follows the breath, it connects with the sensation of the body.

Mind you, the whole process of meditation makes you go through a process, and gradually, you move inward.

The flow of life is such that, once you give the direction to life, it begins to move in that direction. If you switch the direction of life, it takes a while for life energy to be adjusted to the direction, but once the things are adjusted, you effortlessly move along the path.

After the flow of breath, you get in tune with the sensation. You know the inflow and outflow of breath and you know the sensation, but you have never experienced your breath and sensation, the way you will experience now in meditation.

When you put your mind with the inflow and outflow of breathe and observe the depth of the breath, only then for the first time, you really experience your breath. After the breath, you will connect with the sensation. Just to experience the live sensation in the body is altogether a different experience. You have never experienced yourself before until you consciously experience your sensation in the body.

Once you experience the breath and sensation in the body, for the first time you realize, what does it mean to connect with the internal reality?

The inward attention begins with the inflow and outflow of breath and as the flow of breath takes you inward, different facets of your inner world are realized, in the process of meditation.

Once your mind can observe the sensation, slowly your attention will rise higher with the sensation. The attention on the inflow of breath will connect you with the sensation and further by observing the sensation, you rise higher in your inner world.

All the experiences of life limit itself with the sensation. You only experience life with the sensation. You only experience the body as a part of you because of the sensation. It's the sensation that makes you feel alive.

As your attention shifts higher, following the sensation you come across the sex centre. As the sex centre, all your desires related to the sex centre will come to the surface. When your mind will be disconnected from the outside reality and all your energy will be focused inside, all your inner desires will be clearly visible on the surface of the mind.

As your attention will shift higher to the navel region, all your fear, and anxiety related to life will come to the surface. You will be able to experience everything alive on the screen of your mind.

Your role with the mind will be limited to an observer. If you don't engage with the desires at different centres, all the inner desires will be visible to you, and you will surpass them, just as an observer watching the movie on the screen.

When your attention rises from the stomach centre to the heart centre, your feelings, and emotions will be experienced with great intensity. No matter what feelings and emotions, you have held in the moment, either positive or negative will be experienced with greater intensity.

To go through the whole process of meditation is not the work of a day or two, but it's the complete process of transcendence. After the whole process of meditation, you will not remain the same person, who initiated into the process.

The attention of the mind from the heart centre will take you to the throat centre. At every centre of the body, there will be a halt. The energy will not shift higher, before the cleansing process.

The throat centre is the space, where the words are formed. You speak from the throat centre. The throat centre is choked up with all the negative energy that doesn't allow you to speak your truth. You can only express yourself clearly, once you have a clear throat centre.

From the throat centre, your attention will move to the mental region. Remember everything that you experience inside, will only be experienced with the sensation. It's the sensation that will allow you to experience your different centres.

At the mental region, all the experiences and impressions of the past will be viewed with absolute clarity. No part of your mind will be hidden from you. Slowly the attention of the mind will move to the point of attention itself.

The process of thoughts and imagination takes place in the forehead region, but the point of attention is experienced when you rise higher into space, where no thoughts or imagination takes place.

This space is the space from where the mind puts its focus on the internal and external process of life. This space is also known as no-mind state or nothingness of the mind.

Once the attention of the mind moves back to the point of origin, you only feel the sensation at the point of attention. All the external and internal reality is left behind and all you experience is the point of attention.

It takes a while, to experience the no-mind state with the practice of meditation. At the no-mind state, you come to the origin of attention. From this space, nothing remains for you to observe, but your attention becomes standstill in the no-mind state.

Until this space, you observe the sensation and experience all the different centres of your body, but to experience life beyond this state, you have to hold yourself to this state. Kundalini energy or life energy or spirit is experienced, from this space.

This is the doorway to the higher world or the world of energy and vibrations. A new reality opens up for you, once you unlock the life energy inside. Remember the doorway to the higher world is not forward but backward. With the outward attention, you move forward, but with inward attention, you move backward. Your attention moves deeper in you.

Now you wanted to know, how to opens up the life energy, but before you experience the life energy you experience the mind.

When you observe the external reality through your senses or you observe the internal world, you observe with the mind.

When the life energy unlocks inside you experience the whole mind. The point of attention that allows you to observe the external and internal world is part of the mind and when the life energy gets unlocked inside, you realize the whole mind. It's the subtle thread of the life energy that ties the subtle mind to the physical body.

The mind is a separate body that exists in the physical body and it can be experienced, once the life energy is unlocked inside.

In the process of meditation, you remain attentive about the external and internal world. When you take your attention inward, at the most, you can only reach the point of attention itself, and then you have to wait for the inner energy to explode. As the life energy explodes, you experience the whole mind along with the life energy.

The whole mind is experienced first, and in the whole mind you experiences the life energy. Now before we see the nature of life energy, let see the nature of the whole mind, i.e. the mind as a reflective mirror.

5. The Mind is a Reflective Mirror

The mind is a reflective mirror. Now it doesn't need much intelligence to understand the reflective mirror, but to experience your mind as a reflective mirror may take a lifetime.

For the enlightened being, the mind becomes the mirror that reflects both the external and internal reality in its natural form.

When the mind is engaged in the external reality, all it can see is the external world. The inner world remains hidden from the mind. You never even realize that, something more lies in you beneath the mind.

Even the nature of the mind doesn't seem clear, if the mind is engaged in the external reality all the time. When the mind is engaged in the external world, anything that is perceived by the mind is captured in the mind.

All the impressions that are captured by the mind take a form of dreams and desires. Later when your mind forms a desire, you spend your life chasing those desires, but never try to understand the formation of the desires.

No matter what you think or imagine in your mind, is part of the external reality. The mind has captured those images in the form of impressions, somewhere in the past.

If your life remains limited in forming and chasing your desires, you will never come closer to life. Until the mind is engaged in the external reality, the truth of life can never be revealed to you.

The external reality is no more than the effect of life, the cause of which exists inside of you. You need to direct the mind inward, to know the cause behind the external reality, only then the whole truth will be realized by you.

When it comes to the mind, we realize that, the role of the mind is to think thoughts, and imagine things. Dreams and desires are part of the mind. Many consider brain and mind to be the same thing. But when you take your attention inward and experience it for yourself, you will realize that all the thinking, imagination, dreams and desires are certainly part of the mind, but everything that is part of the mind only exists because you have accumulated everything inside from outside.

The mind at its purest form is just the reflective mirror. The mind is plain white clothing that covers your physical body from within.

The mind is a separate subtle body other than the physical body. The brain is part of the physical body, but the mind is separate from the physical body.

At the time of physical death, or deep spiritual experience, even the mind is separated from the physical body and move into its source. Yes, mind too has its source, and the mind is not the absolute truth of life.

When you realize the pure state of mind without any impressions, the movement of life energy or spirit reflects in it. The source of the mind too reflects in the purest state of mind.

Remember the inward journey is all about taking your attention inside. You are very well aware of how to see the external world. In a similar way, when you direct your attention inward, your attention becomes the observer of the inner life.

The observer in you is your purest state of mind. When you see the mirror, what it does?

It reflects.

When you stand in front of the mirror, does the mirror respond or it remain an observer?

The same happens when you direct your attention inward. You don't do anything with the inner process, but you simply observe like a mirror and experience the unfolding of life inside.

You realize the life energy in the mirror of your mind. When the same mind is directed outside, the external reality reflects its true nature, and when you direct the same mind inward, the inner world reflects itself.

You learn the art to observe both the external and internal life, and both the world reflects its true nature in the mirror of your mind.

When you keep your mind engaged with your personal dreams and desires, it remains engaged in chasing your desires, rather understanding the natural process of life. It's only when you drop your own dreams and desires, and simply remain present with life, the life begins to reveal itself to you.

The journey in the external world, simply keeps you engaged with life, while the journey of the inner world, allows you to realize the ultimate truth of life.

The mind is a bridge between the external reality and the higher world. With the mind, you experience the external reality and with the same mind, you realize the source of life.

There are different terms like awareness, pure consciousness, higher intelligence, cosmic mind, observer, self all belongs to the pure state of mind.

When you direct your attention inward, you begin to move in the direction of attention itself, i.e. the mind.

When you see the external reality through the senses, the senses merely act as an instrument for the mind to perceive the external reality, and when you simply shut down the senses, and take your attention inward, you begin to move towards the mind.

When you experience the point of attention of the mind, you experience the no-mind state. When you direct your mind inward, and move towards the mind, you rise above your thinking and imagination and land up to the no-mind state. In the no-mind state, no thought or imagination arises, but you simply experience the peace of mind.

Now as I have mentioned above, the mind is a different subtle body in the physical body. The mind can only be experienced as a reflective mirror, if you can experience the mind, as separate from the physical body.

The inner process of life flows this way.

You have the source in the body. The source is a sacred empty space in the brain. The reason I mention brain, here, because everything is happening within the physical body.

In the physical body exists the subtle body that can be consciously separated by practicing meditation.

The process of life initiates from the source. From the source come the life energy and the mind and enters the physical body to experience life. The pure state of mind is part of the source, and enters the body as subtle clothing, that covers the body from within.

Say, here are the subtle thread of the life energy, the mind in between, and then the main nerves of the physical body.

The mind is subtle clothing that covers the physical body inside. The life energy doesn't directly indulge with the main nerves of the body. The life energy interacts with the main nerves of the body, and the mind stays in between.

Say for e.g., Consider a rope as a spirit or life energy. You have a white plain cloth as a mind, and a physical stick, as main nerves of the body.

Now, here is the rope, the white plain cloth and the physical stick. The white plain cloth covers the physical stick. The rope nourishes the physical stick, while the stick is covered with the white cloth. The rope doesn't directly interact with the stick, but it only works with the cloth.

Remember the mind is a reflective mirror and it will reflect everything that happens inside.

Until you are lost in the thoughts and imagination of the mind, you always distance yourself with the natural process of life. The life doesn't happen with the thoughts and imagination, but it's the work of the life energy that allows the mind to form thoughts and imagination.

The quality of the thoughts and images of the mind depends on the movement of inner life energy. You have noticed the mood swings. The positive or negative thought patterns, or good or bad feelings, are nothing but the result of the shift of the life energy in the body.

Before you realize the mind as a reflective mirror, it's necessary for you to understand, that when you realize the inner life, it's not exactly the life that you see in the external world, but it's only the blueprint that you experience in your inner world.

If you move in the inner world, there are fair chances of you, to look for the similar experiences that you experience in the outside world, but that's not the case.

If you look for the similar experiences as the external world, you may again fooled by your mind. When you take your attention inward, prepare to experience the whole new world that you are not familiar with. Don't try to look for what you have already known in the outside world, or the information that you have gathered about the inner world, otherwise, again you will get caught up in the trap of the subtle world.

The inner world is all about nothingness. This nothingness in you holds all the magic and mysteries of life.

It's hard for the mind to adjust to something that is absolutely empty. The mind only likes to remain full. Whenever it feels empty inside, it moves towards the things that fills the mind from within. One thing that you need to get familiar with is the emptiness of the mind. Initially, it will take some time to adjust, but once you understand the importance of emptiness of the mind, your life will be no less than a miracle.

It's the emptiness of the mind, where the life begins to reflect. The life energy or spirit reflects in the emptiness of the mind. When the mind becomes absolutely empty, all the movement of the life energy gets registered in the mind. It's the natural movement of life energy that allows the mind to connect with the natural process of life. Let see, how the spirit or life energy works in the body.

6. The Experience of Life Energy or Spirit

The experience of life energy is not possible, without experiencing the no-mind state. All your thoughts, imagination, dreams, desires will take you nowhere, but with the emptiness of the mind, you can certainly serve the need of the daily life and overcome all the hurdles of life.

You might have heard about the spirit or life energy or you have some information or knowledge about it. Here you will find the direct experience of life energy.

Life is hard to believe beyond the experiences of the mind, but just beneath the mind lies the life energy or spirit. The life energy in you is a direct experience, the way you experience different facets of life.

The mountain is your experience, the ocean is your experience, the sky is your experience, the sun, moon, and stars are all into your experience. The spirit or life energy too is a similar experience but an internal one.

The mind remains engage in the external reality and the life energy fulfils all the desires of the mind, by working through the body. You go on chasing different desires of the mind, and as you accomplish one desire of the mind, thousands of desires are already waiting outside, to enter in you, and become your internal desire.

If your interest only lies in fulfilling your desires, then the experience of the life energy will be a distant dream for you. When you create the external desire, it's only the life energy that works through the body to bring that desire into reality.

The life energy can be experienced, when you pull your mind from the external desires and direct it inward to realize the absolute truth of life.

When you stop chasing the desires, the life energy that works with the body to manifest the desire, move towards its source. To realize the life energy, is to realize the source that manifests the desires into physical reality.

It all depends on what you desire with life. If you have a longing for truth, you have the same mind that takes you towards the truth, and if you have longing for the external reality, the same mind can keep you engaged with the external reality. The mind remains the same, but it's your desires that change the direction of life.

The life energy or spirit is considered the passive part of the body. Until you have realized the spirit in the body, the spirit is only remained as a constant entity for the mind. If the mind cannot realize the truth about the thing, it makes its own beliefs about the things and this adds illusion to life.

The spirit or life energy is the only active thing in the body. The life energy is constantly moving in the body, taking care of every minute functions within the body. Unless you experience the spirit in the body, it's not possible to grasp the truth behind it.

Remember the physical body cannot nourish itself on its own. The life energy works with the main nerves of the physical body to nourish the whole body. The main nerve of the physical body is directly connected with all parts of the body and once the main nerves of the physical body is nourished, the whole physical system is nourished.

The life energy or spirit in every individual exists in the body as a neutral force. The role of the life energy is to serve the mind and nourish the physical body. The life energy simply follows the natural process of nourishment for the body.

You can fill in, anything you want in your stomach, and then it's the role of the life energy to connect with the main nerves of the body to digest the food.

You can create any desire in the mind, and it's the life energy that works with the body to manifest that desire into life.

Life energy simply follows the mind. The mind can think and imagine anything and the life energy works through the body to manifest the desires of the mind.

The reason it takes time for the life energy to manifest the desire because we cannot hold our mind to one desire. Our mind likes to create different desires at the same time and thus we break the flow of life energy and fail to manifest our desire.

If we can hold one desire at a time, it will be easier for the life energy to manifest that desire with the mind and body.

The only problem with the mind is, unless the mind understands the natural process of life, it cannot make good use of the life energy.

In the external world, you can manifest anything you desire with life, but you need to know the natural process of life. Once you understand the natural flow of life, all you have to do is, create your desire, and become one with the natural flow of life and soon you will see the manifestation of it, in the external reality.

The life energy has its natural movement in the body. The life energy too has its source in the body. The life energy connects with the main nerves of the body, either to nourish the body or to transcend the desire of the mind into reality.

When you direct your mind inward, life energy that has been previously directed to manifest the desires, begin to slip backward.

When the mind begins to understand the natural movement of life energy, it also understands the natural process of life.

The life energy too has its source in the body, and when the mind and body are in absolutely relaxed state, the life energy moves towards its source. That's the reason in the deep meditative state; you experience the state of Samadhi.

The state of Samadhi is experienced when the life energy moves towards its source. The life energy and the mind hold the same source. In a deep meditative state, it's not only the life energy that moves towards its source, but even the mind too moves with the life energy into the source. When the life energy and the mind completely merge into the source that's when you experience the pure state of Samadhi.

The experience of the state of Samadhi is just like falling of a drop into the ocean. When you realize your inner world, you understand that you are no more than a drop. It's the drop that expands itself to experience different colours of life and when the drop moves into the source, it loses its identity and merges into the ocean.

Your physical body grows and develops over the time. Each day you eat and sleep to nourish the body. The mind and spirit in you is a separate subtle body that is no larger than a single drop. The spirit as a subtle thread is a small rope that expands itself to serve the mind and body and when it moves back to the source, it contracts itself similar to a point of dot.

The mind too is a piece of subtle clothing that expands itself to cover the whole physical body from inside, and when it moves towards the source, the subtle cloth too squeezes itself to the size that appears to be no more than a point of a dot.

The experience of the spirit and the mind is real and once you realize the spirit or life energy in the body, you can never move your attention away from the spirit. With the realization of the spirit, the individual identity of the mind is dropped, and the spirit directly begins to live with the mind and body.

With the realization of the spirit, the mind and body work according to the ways of the spirit. The real transcendence of life happens only with the realization of the spirit.

The external world, i.e. the material world, follows certain rules and regulations, which is essential for the smooth flow of the outside world, while the internal life, i.e. the life energy follows the natural process of life that connects you with the eternal process in this very moment. You have to strike a right balance, between the external and internal life.

The mind is a bridge between the internal world and the external world. The internal world here is the world, beneath the mind and not the surface reality of the mind, i.e. your thinking, or imagination, or accumulated experiences and impressions of the outside world.

It's your external world that forms your surface reality of your mind, and later when you create desires out of your inner world, you experience the same desires in the external reality and this forms a vicious circle of life.

The external world forms the inner world and the inner world is experienced in the external world, and the circle of life is formed.

The experience of the life energy takes you beyond the repetitive circle of life and you connect with the eternal circle of life.

80

The life is not a problem, but your understanding towards life is a problem. The life that is happening is something else, and you understand it something else.

When you understand life out of your understanding, you interpret it in your way and go through all the pain, suffering, stress, and anxiety of life.

Once you understand, how life is happening in you, you also understand the external process of life. Once the life is clear to you, you don't struggle with life, but you become one with the natural flow of life. Then no stress, pain, suffering, or anxiety remains for you, but you experience the bliss of life with every breath.

The realization of life energy serves you to understand the natural process of life, but with the realization of the source of life energy or spirit, you experience the creator of life in you.

Your experience doesn't end with the realization of life energy but you experience the ultimate when you experience the source of life energy in you.

7. The Realization of Source

The source is the space in you, from where the life comes. The source of life can be realized within. The realization of the source takes you from an individual mind to the whole mind. The journey towards the source is moving from an individual mind to the whole mind.

Life is experienced out of perception. You have your individual perception to experience life. You have a choice to drop the individual perception and experience the perception of the whole. The realization of the source, allows you to experience life as a whole.

With the mind, the life is a division. The life is not divided, but when you carry your individual perception towards life, it appears to be divided. It's your own dreams and desires that divides life. Division is in your perception.

With the realization of the source, life becomes clear to you. You understand the very process of life. You see how life unfolds in you, and notice that, the life unfolds outside in a similar way.

With life, there is nothing-called chance, luck, or fate, but everything that manifests in the physical world, or that which you experience in your subtle world, comes out of a well-defined process.

Life works at the level of energy. The realization of the source in you connects you with the life energy. The life energy and the mind are part of the source.

There is only one way to realize the source, i.e. from within. The path is only one. As Jesus Christ rightly described to his disciples, that gateway to the heaven is within. Jesus Christ described the source as heaven.

84

Life evolves in you not with the brain and body, but with the awareness of the mind. The more you take your attention deeper, the more life becomes clear to you. The inner attention brings you closer to the source.

The source in you is the space from which the life comes in. With the outside attention, you see the physical manifestation of life, including earth, sky, air, water, and different elements that support life on earth. The natural reality that is perceived by the mind comes out of a definite process.

You too have the earth in you in the form of a physical body. Your body have the water in an equal proportion of the water available on earth. You have a constant flow of breath in the body. You too have the empty space; like a sky and you also have the life energy that is not only creating all the natural elements of the existence but also maintain a perfect balance of earth, water, air and sky in you.

When it comes to the natural aspect of life, you do nothing.

What happens when you realize the source?

With the mind, life is never known to you, and thus you follow your individual mind. However, when you realize the source, you realize the natural process of life that is happening not in the universe but also in you. You align every aspect of life closer to the natural process of life.

After the realization of the source, your daily life doesn't come out of your personal desire, but you make sure to align every aspect of life closer to the natural process of life.

With the mind, life is an illusion.

What is an illusion?

86

The illusion is the story of your mind. Your mind doesn't think in terms of action, but your mind thinks in terms of the result you may arrive, out of the action. You go on thinking about the past and the future and slips away from this moment. It may appear with the individual mind that you are living the present life but that's not the case.

Life unfolds out of its natural process, no matter what kind of illusion you savour in your mind. That's the only reason; your thinking never matches the present reality of life. You always think something else and life always appears something else. Life surprises you every moment.

Let me tell you, there is no surprise with life and life is simply following its process. However, with the individual mind, the reality never appears in its true colours, because you only see what your mind wants you to see. One thing needs to be clear to the mind, that unless the source of life is realized, both the external and internal reality will remain a puzzle. It's only with the realization of the source, the mystery of life is revealed to you.

The god that exists in the external reality is the product of the mind. When the mind doesn't understand something, it simply puts into a category, of god, mystery, luck, fate or chance, but never try to get behind the truth of it. When you look for the truth in life, you always realize the truth, beyond your individual beliefs and perception about life.

There is no way to understand life just with your faith and beliefs. Your faith and beliefs will note take you too far, but eventually you have to search for the truth.

People don't consider god and life to be one. They think both as a two separate thing. It's only at the time of problem they look for god when life seems to slip out of hand. The mind has its limitations. The mind can only think and imagine things that are in his experience. Beyond the personal experience, the mind becomes helpless.

The mind can only control that it knows, but every moment life is happening fresh. The actions from the mind thinking about the past and the future, while the present moment unfolds out of its natural process and thus the contrast remain behind the life with the mind, and the life that unfolds outside.

Unless the mind works to understand the ways of life, the life will always remain mystery for the mind.

The god and life are one. By realizing the source in you, you realize the god and its creation. The creation of life is an ever-going process. The life is happening all the time. To

realize the source of life and to realize the truth
you have to move inward.

It's only when you move inward, and travel
the inner path, you realize the source of life, and
only by knowing the source of life, you know that
which needs to be known with life and you attain
that ultimate beyond which nothing remains for
you to attain.

Life doesn't end with the realization of a
source, but you develop altogether a different
perception towards life. With the expanded
perception you directly look into life, and
experience life, not in the past or the future but
in this moment.

Life becomes a direct experience with the
realization of the source. Let see how you
experience life after the realization of self.

8. Life after realization of Source

There is a Zen saying, "Before Enlightenment chop wood carry water, after Enlightenment, chop wood carry water."

When you realize the source of life in you, nothing changes and everything change simultaneously. In the outside world nothing changes and in the inner world everything transcends. This is the beauty of enlightenment. Everything remains the same, but you become different.

You develop the knowing towards life. No knowledge but knowing. You know the source of knowledge. You discover the process of life. You know now, how life works.

It's like, if I ask you, where is the sky? You can directly point me to the sky. No knowledge direct knowing. Life is no knowledge. Life is all about knowing. Once you know, you know forever.

The mind can only create confusion until it knows the very source of life. Once the source of life is known to the mind, the mind itself is dropped. Dropping the mind doesn't mean literally dropping it, but all the knowledge of the mind gets dropped and you directly experience life. You become the witness to life. Your mind becomes an observer to life.

Remember it's the same mind. The mind remains the same. Before enlightenment, you look with the same mind, but with an individual perspective. After the realization, it's the same mind, but now you see life from the perspective of a whole. The mind remains the same, but your perspective to view life transcends from individual too whole.

How does mind look like from inside?

See mind as a plain white piece of cloth, and put your thinking, imagination, dreams, desires, ideas, beliefs, and everything that runs in your mind in that piece of cloth. When you realize the pure state of mind, you can see all the things that exist in the mind. Your mind as a whole looks exactly like white piece of cloth. You lose the individual identity and realize yourself as a white plain cloth, i.e. pure mind. You are that white plain cloth on which everything takes place. You are nothing but the mind.

The mind is not the source of life, but the mind is a different subtle body that exists in the body. The individual identity too is developed on the surface of the mind. When you realize yourself as mind, your individual identity too is left behind.

All your thinking, or imagination, or past or future still moves on the surface of the mind, but you see everything as a detached observer. If you wish, you participate with life and if you wish, you can simply pull out from life, not only from the external world, but also from the subtle world.

After enlightenment, you live with the pure state of mind. You don't follow the activities of the mind, but you arrange your life according to the movement of life energy. You experience life in the moment. You think of the past and the future, but just as a reference point. You cannot get lost into life as an observer.

Space and time can be observed with the pure state of mind. When you are part of the circle of life, your life moves into space and time. Space and mind is a thing of a mind. It only exists in the mind. When you can slip beneath the surface reality of the mind, you move beyond the circle of time and space.

You cannot see space and time, as separate from you, as you exist in your body. With the realization of the self, you can see the circle of time and space both inside and outside life. The time and space exist only on the surface of the mind. If you know, how to consciously slip beneath the surface reality of the mind, you can move beyond the time and space of the mind.

The state of enlightenment gives you clarity with both the inner as well as outside life. You just know how the life works both in the inner as well as outside world. You simply become one with the process of life. Your daily life doesn't reflect the desires, but all it reflects is the natural process of life.

You serve the need of the moment. The mind is so engrossed in the external reality, that it cannot see the truth of life. Unless the mind becomes absolutely empty the life doesn't reflect on it.

The natural state of mind is pure emptiness. Your mind is just a mirror that reflects everything that comes on the mirror of the mind, but when you fill it up with different experiences and impressions of life, you cannot see the natural flow of life, but all you see, is your own experiences and impressions that you have accumulated over the time.

There is no mystery to life. Life is plain simple. It simply follows its natural course. This natural course of life is visible in the mind.

If you are a seeker, or you are interested to know the truth, then you don't have to go far away, but only work to empty your mind.

First, you have to understand, how you have filled your mind. Once you understand how you have filled it up, then it will be easier to empty your mind.

Your daily life fills your mind. With your daily life, not everything is important, but there are very few things, that serve the purpose of life. You have to bring your attention to the daily living. When you become aware of your daily living and live with intent to drop the things, that doesn't serve your daily purpose; your awareness begins to grow in the moment.

With an empty mind, your awareness is heightened. You can see through life. When your mind is filled with garbage, you only perceive life out of the garbage.

Life is always fresh in the moment. You don't have to live in the past or future of the mind. Life is offering fresh experience all the time.

Say, for e.g., you have stored water in a tank and you only make use of that stored water. On the other hand, you have a tap that can give you fresh water, anytime you open the tap.

Which one you prefer?

Life is offering fresh experience all the time. The fresh experience of the moment connects you with the eternal circle of life. You don't have to worry about your past or the future, but when you connect with the present moment, your past and future is taken care of in the moment.

All your efforts need to be directed not in accumulating the experiences and impressions of life, rather becoming an observer of life. An observer doesn't run after the desires of life, but simply remain present with life, and allow the life to unfold on its own. You serve the need of the day and become the observer of life. You don't indulge yourself with unnecessary things.

The realization of source happens by emptying the mind and not filling it up. When the emptiness becomes the goal of your life, all your choice, and decisions comes out of conscious mind. You only choose the essential. You serve the need of the moment. More your awareness grows in the moment, more the truth behind the situations of life become clear to you. If your goal remains to empty your mind, then your every choice and decision will lead you towards your goal.

With life, what matters is your direction. If you direct your life in filling your mind, all your actions will only fill you up and your mind will constantly remain engaged in thinking and imagination.

On the other hand, if you direct your life towards emptiness, then slowly with the process of life you come closer to the source of life.

The life with the source is possible, if you develop intent to move towards the source. The life with the source is not a single experience, but it's your daily living.

With the realization of the source, you live with the source. Your daily living comes directly out of the source. Your daily life becomes one with the natural order of life.

Life is beautiful if enlightenment happens to you. The truth is beautiful only within us. In others, we can have a glimpse of it, but if the existence has made us capable of experiencing the beauty within us, then why not strive to bring that truth, rather remain contented by having a glimpse in others.

Author Bio

The name of the author is Roshan Sharma. He runs a blog under the name https://modernagespirituality.com/ and has written over 400 blogs covering the topics, from God to religion, spirituality, philosophy, mind, psychology, awareness, consciousness, energy, vibrations and many more.

He is a regular practitioner of meditation and an avid reader of life. Everything that is shared in the blog or book is out of inner experience. He has been part of many spiritual organizations but always believed that everything that exists in the outside world in relation to god or the self is only the pointer to the inner truth. The inner truth can only be realized inside by one's own effort.

With life, what's important is, the way you understand life. If your understanding itself goes against the way of life, you can only move away from life rather coming closer to it. The process of life doesn't initiate with the mind, but you have something more exists in you, out of which the process of life happens through you.

Unless you recognize that source in you, from where the process of life initiates, all the chaos and confusion, and stress and suffering will be part of your life. Your daily life has to happen from the source and not with the mind.

The self-realization is the ultimate purpose of life. The process of self-realization is to direct the mind towards the source. With the self-realization, you develop altogether a different perception towards life. You perceive life from the pure state of mind, or you can say the life reflects on your pure state of mind, the way moon reflects in the river. You become the observer of life.

Blog: ModernAgeSpirituality.com

Our journey of life doesn't end with the book. We can remain connected with the blog. If you have any query in relation to the book, or like to share your feedback, or you have some personal or spiritual query to ask, you can reach us through our blog.

On the blog, you will have almost all the topics in relation to life. The blog is not limited to spirituality, but you will find spiritual view for your personal or professional life.

The purpose of the blog is to stay connected with you and share the broader perspective of life.

The wisdom of life is not to reach to the destination, but understand the present moment from the broader perspective. The past and future lies in the moment, and thus if you can have clarity about this moment, you develop clarity with the whole life.

You can also connect with us on our Social Media Platform, please visit the below link:

https://plus.google.com/+RoshanSharma86098

https://www.facebook.com/modernagespirituality?ref=hl

https://twitter.com/ModernAgeSpirit

https://www.instagram.com/modernagespirituality/

To be Continued...

CPSIA information can be obtained
at www.ICGtesting.com
Printed in the USA
LVHW080918271119
638693LV00007BA/123/P